UML AND
OBJECT-ORIENTED DESIGN
FOUNDATIONS

KÁROLY NYISZTOR

CONTENTS

.

CHAPTER 1
INTRODUCTION

Thank you for your interest in my book UML and Object-Oriented Design Foundations.

This book is going to teach you fundamental knowledge needed to design and build object-oriented software systems.

WHY SHOULD YOU LEARN OBJECT-ORIENTED DESIGN?

The main goal of this book is to avoid the situation when you stare at your favorite IDE without knowing what to do next.

After learning the basic syntax of a programming language, we start writing some code. Eventually, we realize that creating real-world applications requires additional skills.

Mastering the syntax of a programming language is not enough. We must also know how to design a software system by applying common object-oriented programming principles. And we must be able to describe our design so that others can understand it clearly.

Besides, you'll probably come across object-orientation related questions during job interviews.

This book is about object-oriented software design related concepts and the Unified Modeling Language. The Unified Modeling Language - in short UML - provides a standard set of visual symbols and diagramming techniques used to effectively communicate software design concepts. Using UML we can sketch our systems easily.

The steps required to create a software system are not carved in stone. Yet, attempts have been made to formalize the process. These are known as software development methodologies. We're going to discuss two widespread methodologies in this book.

Object-orientation has been around since the 80's, but its principles are still valid and used in modern software design. I dedicated an entire section to the fundamental object-orientation concepts.

Next, you'll learn about the various steps of the object-oriented software analysis and design process. Mastering these techniques will let you design your software systems more efficiently.

Then, we'll dive into UML. I'll talk about the core UML notions and the fundamental UML diagram types.

I'm going to talk about use cases, the primary way of describing the requirements in a formal way.

I'll introduce you the class diagram, which lets us describe the main types that form a system and the relationships between them.

We'll then talk about sequence diagrams, which are the way to go if you want to represent the dynamic behavior of your objects. We'll also have a look at the activity and the state diagram.

After discussing the most important UML diagram types, we'll solidify the concepts you learned. I'm going to walk you through the steps of designing a note taking application from scratch.

We'll start by collecting the requirements. Then, we'll create the use case diagrams. After identifying the players, we'll model the classes and their relationships. You're going to also see the sequence and the state diagram in action.

SECTION 1.3
PREREQUISITES

This book is beginner-friendly. I explain each concept clearly and illustrate it using practical examples.   So, you don't have to be an expert by any means, but you should have at least fundamental programming knowledge.   I'll be using basic ideas like for example conditions, methods, attributes, and I assume you understand them.

Download StarUML if you want to follow along with me the creation of the UML diagrams in this book. It is available for Mac, Linux and Windows at www.staruml.io.

Although we won't be writing any source code, I'll show you some code examples. I use Atom, a free and open-source text and source code editor developed by GitHub. It is available on www.atom.io and it runs on macOS, Linux, and Microsoft Windows.

Also, you can visit my website http://www.leakka.com and my Youtube channel https://www.youtube.com/c/swiftprogrammingtutorials where you can find many programming related articles and video tutorials.

CHAPTER 2
SOFTWARE DEVELOPMENT METHODOLOGIES

There are different ways to develop a software system. Sure, you can just sit down and start typing source code. This works until, well, it doesn't.

For anything more complicated than a Hello World app, you'll need a way to organize your work. And if you're not working alone, the lack of a (reasonably) well-defined process is going to lead to chaos.

As the complexity of a project and the number of involved people increases, the need for a development process becomes more and more prevalent.

Different approaches have been invented. We're going to talk about two of the most popular development methodologies, namely:

The Waterfall model, which requires you to have a detailed plan before starting any coding. The requirements need to be fixed, so no changes are expected during development.

The change-friendly, responsive Agile approach, which works great for projects where the expectations can change rapidly and frequently.

Before we delve into these methodologies, I must tell you one thing:

None of these systems can precisely describe every step of the software development process.

But we definitely need them to synchronize and organize our development related activities; activities that include not only coding but also design, product management, budgeting, testing, documentation, release and maintenance.

SECTION 2.1
THE WATERFALL MODEL

The Waterfall is a linear model. It defines development steps or phases. You start executing one step, complete it and then start the next one. This approach gives us a steady, downward order. Hence the name Waterfall.

The development process flows in cascades. Each development phase requires the previous one to be completed. Let's talk a bit about these phases.

First, we **collect and analyze the requirements**. The expected functionality of the future application must be clarified with the stakeholders. All the details must be documented thoroughly. This very first phase is probably the most important one. When done right, the Waterfall model will produce the expected outcome.

After collecting and analyzing the requirements, we can proceed to the next phase. Here's where we **define the overall design** of our software. Defining the architecture is like creating the blueprint for a building. Thus, the design should be as clear and detailed as possible. The bottom line is this: the team should be able to implement the product based on this plan. We should address questions like:

- *Which packages or components will form our system?*
- *What are the fundamental types of each component?*
- *How do these types interact with each other to achieve the required functionality?*
- *Is our software secure? How about performance?*
- *How does our software respond to errors? How do we handle edge cases?*
- *Should we extend our system in the future?*
- *Which third-party components do we use?*

The list can grow or shrink depending on the requirements we defined in the previous phase.

The implementation comes next. The **software development phase** is usually divided into smaller units. Each unit is then implemented and tested by developers.

Once the development phase is completed, the product undergoes the **verification phase**. During this step, the software is evaluated based on predefined criteria. We must check whether the product provides the functionality we agreed on.

Tests are executed to ensure that the software works as expected. We test for functional, performance, security and usability issues. Detected problems are recorded and fixed. The process goes on until all severe bugs are fixed.

The verification phase may also bring to surface deeper bugs and critical issues that may affect the planned release.

As soon as the testing phase completes and the given version is delivered, the software enters the **maintenance phase**. By definition, the maintenance phase is about fixing smaller bugs. But more often than not, it may also include functional enhancements.

The client may come up with new requirements that involve substantial changes. You may feel tempted to squeeze in "just one more patch" in the maintenance phase. This is usually a bad idea. In this case, we need to set up a new waterfall project and repeat all the steps.

The following figure shows the phases of the Waterfall model:

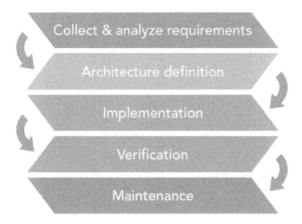

The Waterfall model is used for life-control, medical and military systems. This model requires us to clarify all the requirements and create a detailed plan upfront.

The Waterfall is a perfect choice if all requirements are precisely defined and won't change over time. The Waterfall has received some criticism for its inability to respond to changes. Due to its linear structure, new requirements can't be considered at later phases of the development process.

If the client changes their mind frequently, or our design misses essential aspects, we're going to hit problems during development or testing. In such cases, we should follow a different approach.

SECTION 2.2
AGILE

Agile is a relatively new approach to software project management. It all began with the agile manifesto in 2001. This manifesto was an attempt to end the proliferation of methodologies that had developed.

The agile manifesto defines four values:

- **Individuals and interactions over the processes and tools**
  This doesn't mean that we won't use processes and tools in agile projects. We still need tools and processes, but they shouldn't prevent us from implementing the required features or changes.
  Instead of enforcing people to follow a rigid process, we implement a process that's adaptive and responds to changes.
- **Working software over comprehensive documentation**
  This doesn't mean that agile projects don't use documentation at all. We should create documentation where it provides value. There's no need to create extensive documentation just for the sake of it.
- **Customer collaboration over contract negotiation**
  Don't get this wrong either. Agile projects also require contracts to manage customer expectations about costs and schedules. Yet, unlike for plan driven projects, there is a spirit of partnership between the development team and the customer. Due to the somewhat uncertain nature of agile projects, both parties acknowledge that some requirements and details may need to be redefined or clarified further as the project progresses. It goes without saying that this kind of partnership requires collaboration and trust.
- **Responding to change over following a plan**
  Agile is different from plan driven approaches and provides more flexibility compared to the Waterfall model. The major difference is that agile welcomes changes even at the later phases of the

development cycle. Some planning is also required for agile projects. But we don't try to come up with a detailed plan for the entire project before starting any development activities. As a consequence we're not blocked until all the requirements are clarified and each and every question gets answered.

Now let's talk about how an Agile approach solves the problem we saw with the Waterfall.

The main idea behind Agile is that we can provide functional software iteratively instead of delivering the entire project all at once. The work is broken up into shorter chunks called sprints.

The Sprint is usually two to four weeks long. At the end of each sprint the team should deliver a version that's an improvement over the previous sprint's outcome.

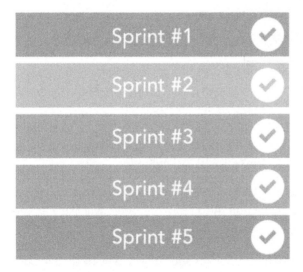

This interactive approach provides an opportunity to frequently review the product that's being developed. Stakeholders have a chance to evaluate the software and provide their feedback early on rather than waiting for the final product to be delivered. These frequent checkpoints are super useful as they ensure that the project evolves in the right direction.

Unlike the waterfall, agile methodologies do not separate testing from development. Testing is tightly integrated with development and the entire team owns the responsibility for the quality of the product. Also involving the business users in the development process stands at the core of agile approaches.

There's a strong relationship between the project team and the stakeholders and business users. This model works best in situations where the requirements can't be defined upfront.

Agile is a good fit for software projects that are depending on many uncertain factors and changes are to be expected.

One of the big benefits of this collaborative model is that it usually leads to higher customer satisfaction. Also team members will likely be more motivated by engaging customers directly.

Note that Agile is not a methodology but rather a way of thinking defined by the agile manifesto values and principles.

Agile is a way of thinking.

Scrum and Kanban are examples of discrete methodologies that implement the Agile approach.

Waterfall is usually perceived as rigid and bureaucratic compared to Agile methodologies. However, both have their place.

There are cases where a plan driven methodology won't work. If the level of uncertainty is high and not all questions can be answered right away, then you should probably choose an agile methodology. For other projects, a waterfall-like approach will be a better fit.

Let me give you some examples.

When developing a weapons control system, the requirements should be clarified in advance and need to be stable. Changing the requirements midway would increase the costs considerably and these kinds of projects are expensive anyway. A Waterfall approach makes perfect sense in this case.

Here's another (real) example from Upwork:

"Looking to create the next big social media platform for IOS and Android"

Coming up with a detailed plan based on assumptions wouldn't make sense. The description is vague, and the customer won't be able to describe precisely what they need. This high level of uncertainty calls for an agile approach. Creating "the next big social network" will require multiple iterations.

So, to sum it up you should use the Waterfall when you know what the final product should be, and clients can't change the scope of the project.

Agile methodologies should be used when there's a lot of uncertainty involved, the requirements are vague or rapidly changing and clients can't precisely describe what the end-product should do or look like.

CHAPTER 3
CORE OBJECT-ORIENTATION CONCEPTS

This Dilbert comic walks us through the history of programming. It's a bit of an exaggeration, but programming was totally different a couple of decades ago.

Nowadays it is easy to get started with programming. There are various visual tools and sophisticated development environments that make learning fun.

We can program drones and robots, create 3D-games or augmented reality apps. We can achieve all that without having to learn for years. We're lucky to have all these great tools today.

1950	1960	1980
Non-structured programming	Structured programming	Object-Oriented programming

Initially, computer programs were big, contiguous chunks of code. The **unstructured programming** was the earliest programming paradigm. The code consisted of sequentially ordered instructions. Each statement would go in a new line. Source code lines were numbered or identified by a label.

Here's an example written in Sinclair Basic. This simple program converts from Fahrenheit to Celsius degrees:

```
10 PRINT "Fahrenheit", "Celsius"
20 PRINT
30 INPUT "Enter deg F", F
40 PRINT F, (F-32)*5/9
50 GO TO 30
```

As the programs grew in complexity, the drawbacks of this approach had become apparent. Maintaining or even understanding such a code base was challenging. To make any changes or improvements, you had to check the statements line by line.

This task becomes more and more difficult as the number of code lines increases. Non-structured programming was heavily criticized for producing hardly readable, so-called "spaghetti" code.

The term spaghetti code is a pejorative description for complicated, difficult to understand, and impossible to maintain, software.

Structured programming emerged in the late 50s.
Structured programming languages break down code into logical steps. They rely on subroutines, which contain a set of instructions to be carried out. Here's an example of a program written in C, which is a procedural language:

```
#include<stdio.h>
int sum(int, int);
int main()
{
```

```c
int x, y;
int sum;

printf("Enter the first integer number: ");
scanf("%d", &x);

printf("Enter the second integer number: ");
scanf("%d", &y);

sum = sum(x, y);

printf("x: %d, y: %d\n", x, y);
printf("Sum: %d\n", sum);

return 0;
}

int sum(int x,int y)
{
   int sum;
   sum = x + y;
   return sum;
}
```

The function called *main()* is the entry point of our program. It calls the *sum()* function to add the two numbers entered by the user.

We can define additional methods. For example, if we need to calculate the average of the two numbers, we could create a function like this:

```c
float average(float x, float y)
{
   return (x + y) / 2;
}
```

These subroutines operate on variables and data structures.

A variable represents a value of a given type that can be identified using a name.

```c
int x, y;
float salary;
```

We use the name of the variable to access the stored value. This lets us modify the value during runtime.

```c
int x = 10 // x has a value of 10
x = 42 // x is now 42
```

```
x = x + 1 // x is now 43
```

A data structure is a way of organizing and storing data in a computer program. Here's a structure that aggregates the information needed to represent an employee:

```
struct employee {
    int identifier;
    char name[30];
    float salary;
};
```

Structured programming was a significant improvement compared to the monolithic coding practices. Named functions improved the readability of the computer programs. The development time could be reduced substantially.

Even with the improved quality, developers started to face new challenges as the programs got bigger and bigger. Structured programming could not address all the increased complexity.

Object-orientation was the next big step in the evolution of the programming paradigms. Object-oriented languages appeared in the 80s. The main idea was to split apart the program into self-contained objects. Each object represents a part of the system that gets mapped to a distinct entity. Basically, an object functions as a separate program by itself. It operates on its own data and has a specific role.

The objects that form the system interact with each other. Object-orientation aims to bring the world of programming closer to the real world.

SECTION 3.1
OBJECTS

While structured programming relies on actions, object-oriented programming is organized around objects.

An object represents a thing. Just like in real life, objects can be simple or complex.

A golf ball is an object, but so is Falcon Heavy. The way we define the object depends on the level of detail we need.

With the launch of the Falcon Heavy, they also sent the Tesla Roadster with "Starman" in the driver's seat toward Mars orbit. Objects may contain or refer to other objects. This can also happen in the object-oriented world.

We can describe objects using their properties. They can have attributes like name, color, weight, velocity. A golf ball can be completely white, colored or it may even glow in the dark. It has a weight and a price. Some properties like its position, speed, and acceleration can change, while other attributes (its color for example) will stay the same.

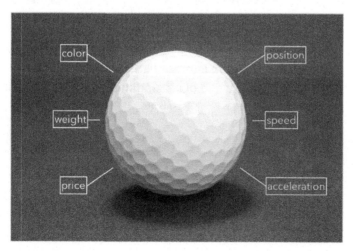

All these properties describe an object in the real world. This approach works also in an object-oriented language.

Objects have their identity, their own state. Changing the state of an object doesn't change the state of other objects. If we hit a golf ball, it won't affect all the other balls. Their state is independent, each has its private identity.

Besides properties and identity, an object has its own behavior. The behavior of an object is what it can do.

"The black dog barks"

In this sentence, we identify one object: **the dog**.
"Bark" is the behavior, or the action performed by the "dog" object. And **"black"** is its color, one of its attributes.

We can identify the object easily since it's the noun in the sentence. The verb is the behavior, and the adjective is the property.

We describe an object using its properties, identity, and behavior.

Quite straightforward, but how do we make this work in our code? For that, we need to introduce a new concept, the class.

Building an object-oriented system starts by identifying the potential objects, their attributes, and responsibilities. We need to have a class before we can create an object.

The class is the blueprint of an object.

You can think of a class as a plan, a description of what an object will be. An object is a realization of this blueprint.

Let's say you want to use a Pokémon in your program. A class called *Pokémon* would provide a blueprint for what the Pokémon looks like and what it can do.

The class tells us that each object has a name, armor level and hit points. It doesn't say what the name or the armor level is.

A Pokémon can attack, and it can defend itself. These two actions define its behavior.

properties

   name

   armor

   hit points

actions

   attack

   defend

We created a class by giving it a name, declaring its properties and actions. We call these actions methods. Methods are blocks of code that can be called to execute certain operations. They may take input parameters and can also return values. Methods are like functions in structured programming languages. The methods are basically functions embedded in a class.

Given this class, we can create objects based on it. Upon object creation, we provide the values for the attributes declared in the class. Each object will have a name, armor level and hit points. The *attack()* and *defend()* behavior is provided by the class.

Given a blueprint, we can create as many instances as we need.

Another big benefit of classes is that we can package them into libraries or frameworks. This lets us reuse them in other programs as well.

All modern object-oriented programming languages provide such built-in frameworks. We don't have to reinvent the wheel and implement the functionality that's readily available. Instead, we can focus on creating and using the objects in our programs.

Now each program has different requirements. The pre-made classes will rarely cover all our needs. You'll often find yourself creating your own classes.

We covered the object and the class. Next, we'll take a look at the core object-orientation principles.

ABSTRACTION

Abstraction is a way of describing complex problems in simple terms, by ignoring some details. Eliminating the nitty-gritty details let us focus on the bigger picture. We can dig deeper once we have a broader understanding.

How does abstraction work?

If I say *cat*, you know what I'm talking about. I don't need to say I was thinking of a male Persian cat, if it's a kitten, if it's big or small.

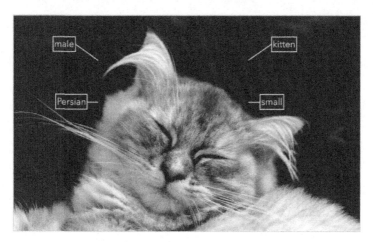

You understand that I was talking about a cat.

We are naturally good at generalizing things. We skip the irrelevant details, but people will still understand us. That's because our brains are wired to understand abstract ideas like cat, house or car.

Abstraction works the same way in the object-oriented world. When we start defining a class, we focus on the essential qualities of that class.

Focus on essential qualities, discard unimportant ones.

Back to our Pokémon example: we started with the most important attributes and methods. We don't need details like age, weight or height,

so we can ignore them.
These attributes are unessential in our current application.

So, that's how abstraction works. We focus on what's important and ignore all the details we don't need.

ENCAPSULATION

The next fundamental idea to keep in mind when dealing with OOP and classes is called **encapsulation**.

We encapsulate something to protect it and keep its parts together. Think of how medicine is enclosed in a shell called capsule.

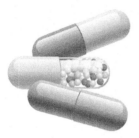

In object-orientation, this translates to packing together our properties and methods in a class. Encapsulation also means hiding the gears and the levers.

Here's an example. We can use a phone without understanding electronics. We don't need to know how the touchscreen, the camera or the logic board works.

Similarly, we don't want to expose the inner workings of our class. An object should only reveal the essential features. This concept is called **data hiding**. By hiding its internal details, the object is protected from external interference.

We restrict clients from modifying the object in ways we did not originally plan, whether it's intentional or accidental. Additionally, we prevent other parts of the system from relying on properties or behavior that may change.

If you replace your phone's battery, that won't affect the way you use your phone. That's because you only interact with the touchscreen.

Changes in the inner workings of your phone don't matter to you. Our classes shouldn't be any different either.

If we expose unnecessary details, any changes to those attributes or methods may affect other parts of the system. Whereas if we restricted access to that data or behavior, we don't have to worry about the ripple effect of our changes.

Data hiding is not about selfishly keeping stuff for ourselves. It's rather about protecting our classes from unwanted external dependencies.

As a rule of thumb:

Expose only as much of your class properties and methods as needed for normal usage.

Data hiding plays an essential role in keeping the dependencies between objects to a minimum.

A tightly coupled system, with most of the objects depending on each other, is the obvious sign of a bad design. Updating or maintaining such a system is a pain. Any tiny modification will cascade down and require you to change other parts of the system, too. It's like a never-ending nightmare.

Object-oriented programming principles are here to make our lives easier. Next up is the idea of Inheritance.

INHERITANCE

Inheritance is a key concept in object-oriented programming. Without inheritance, we'd end up writing similar code over and over again.

Inheritance means code reuse. That is, reusing an existing class implementation in new classes.

Let us start with an example. We modeled the Pokémon class with the main properties and behavior in mind. Given this class, we were able to create our Pokémon instances.

Now, what if we need new types, like *electric, water* or *flying* Pokémon? We will need new classes since these new types have special abilities.

The Pokémon class has the properties name, armor and hit points, and it can attack and defend itself. The Electric, Water and Flying Pokémon have all these properties, and they are also able to attack and defend themselves. Additionally, they also have specialized functionality.

An Electric Pokémon has the ability to *wild charge*. This attack is only available to Electric-type Pokémons. *AquaTail* is a damaging Water Pokémon move, and Flying Pokémons can perform the *dragon ascent* attack.

As you've probably realized, the three new classes are almost identical to the Pokémon class. The only difference is the special attack type.

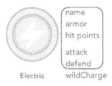

Electric   wildCharge   Water   aquaTail   Flying   dragonAscent

We could add all these new behaviors to the Pokémon class. If we did that, we'd end up in a class that has too many responsibilities. Suddenly, all Pokémon objects could swim and fly and discharge electricity.

We definitely don't want that. Our classes should be simple. They need to have a well-defined purpose.

Object-orientation is about granularity and separation of concerns. Each class should focus on one set of specific functionalities and do that well.

Creating one-size-fits-all, monolithic classes is a major mistake in object-oriented software development.

So, how about keeping these classes separate? That sounds better. But now, we keep repeating the same code for the common functionality. There must be a better way.

Indeed, object-oriented programming languages have a solution for this kind of problem: Inheritance.

A class can inherit all the attributes and behavior from another class. In our case, we let ElectricPokémon, WaterPokémon, and FlyingPokémon inherit from the Pokémon class. The data and the behavior from the Pokémon class are now available to all these classes, without us having to write a single line of code.

Now we can add specialized behavior or attributes to the classes that inherit from Pokémon.

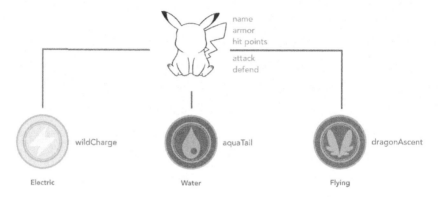

If we enhance or modify the Pokémon class, all the other classes will automatically receive those changes.

In object-oriented terms, Pokémon is a parent or superclass. Whereas the ElectricPokémon, WaterPokémon, and FlyingPokémon are subclasses or child classes.

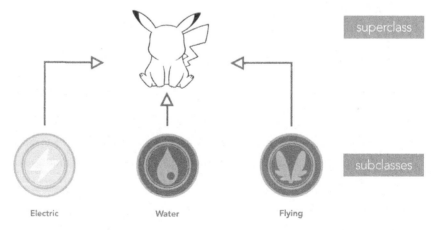

Inheritance is a powerful idea which can save us from a lot of typing. Besides, it paves the road to another handy feature called Polymorphism.

POLYMORPHISM

Here's another term you'll often hear when it comes to object-orientation: Polymorphism.

The word has Greek origins, and it consists of two words: "polys", which means many, much and "morphé," meaning form or shape.

If you look up the word polymorphism, you'll find the following definition:

The condition of occurring in several different forms.

How does this apply to programming?
To understand how polymorphism works, we have to revisit the idea of inheritance.

Here's our Pokémon superclass and its subclasses.

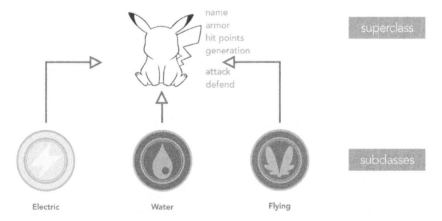

The Electric, Water and FlyingPokémon all inherit the data and the behavior of their superclass. So, they have a name, armor, hit points and they can attack and defend themselves.

The WaterPokémon inherits the attack behavior from the Pokémon superclass. Now, what if we need WaterPokémon types to cause more damage than basic Pokémons?

For that, we need to provide a specialized implementation of the attack behavior. This is what we call method overriding.

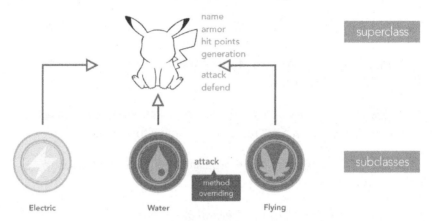

By overriding a method of the superclass, we tell that we want a different behavior in our subclass than the one we inherited.

Method overriding is straightforward: we re-implement the method with the same name and parameters as the one defined in the parent class and provide our own behavior.

By doing so, our WaterPokémon objects will have a different *attack()* behavior than their Pokémon superclass. Calling the *attack()* method on the Electric and Flying Pokémon objects will use the logic implemented in their superclass, since we did not override the *attack()* method in their case.

So, that's method overriding. Polymorphism lets us work with objects created from any of these classes. We don't need to know whether its a Water, Flying or Electric Pokémon instance to call any of the common methods defined in the superclass.

We could create an army of mixed Pokémons and tell them to attack at once.

Each of them will execute the right attack() method without us having to know their exact type. All we know is that they are all instances of the Pokémon type or one of its subclasses.

Polymorphism is about working freely with instances of many different classes that share a common superclass.

It's probably easier to grasp it when using it in a real program, so let me show you an example. I'm going to use Swift and Xcode on a Mac.

We'll implement the Pokémon class and all the subclasses. This is an overly simplified example but it's good enough to show you how polymorphism works in a real program. So, here's our Pokémon class. The *attack()* method just displays a message to the console.

```
class Pokémon {

  var name: String

  init(name: String) {
    self.name = name
  }

  func attack() {
    print("Pokémon attack!")
  }
}
```

The Electric, Water and Flying Pokémon classes inherit from the Pokémon class. This is how we do it in Swift: we put the name of the superclass after the name of the child class separated by a colon.

```
class ElectricPokémon: Pokémon {

}

class WaterPokémon: Pokémon {

}

class FlyingPokémon: Pokémon {

}
```

I override the attack method in the WaterPokémon class. To specify that I'm overriding a method in the superclass I'm using the override keyword. For this example, we'll simply display a different message:

```
class WaterPokémon: Pokémon {
  override func attack() {
    print("WaterPokémon attack!")
  }
}
```

Next, I'll create some Pokémon instances. One Pokémon object, a WaterPokémon, then an Electric and a FlyingPokémon, too.

```
let eevie = Pokémon(name: "Eevie")
let misty = WaterPokémon(name: "Misty")
let pikachu = ElectricPokémon(name: "Pikachu")
let charizard = FlyingPokémon(name: "Charizard")
```

Then, I define a list with these objects. Now, I can traverse this list and call the *attack()* method on the objects in the list. We don't need to know the class they were instantiated from.

```
let pokémons = [eevie, pikachu, misty, charizard]

for pokémon in pokémons {
    pokémon.attack()
}
```

If I run the demo, we'll see in the console that the attack method produced the same output in the console for all the objects but one.

Pokémon attack!

Pokémon attack!

WaterPokémon attack!

Pokémon attack!

That object was of type WaterPokémon, which overrides the attack() method.

CHAPTER 4
OBJECT-ORIENTED ANALYSIS AND DESIGN

Building an object-oriented application requires some preliminary steps. These steps are similar regardless of the development methodology.

First, we need to **collect the requirements**. During the requirements collection phase, we answer the following questions:

- What's the problem we're trying to solve?
- What does our app or framework need to do to accomplish that functionality?

The requirements collection step involves a lot of brainstorming and discussions. Once we come to an agreement, we need to document our ideas. The requirements need to be as clear as possible.

Only write down the decisions that underline what the system is going to do. Vague thoughts will lead to conflicts later on.

Once the requirements are clear, we come up with a **description of the software system**. We should describe the app from the user's perspective.

Depending on the project, we may pick an agile or a waterfall methodology. For agile projects, it is completely fine if we don't provide an accurate description. We can still fill the gaps or refine our thoughts later on. The point here is to gain as much clarity as needed to start the next step.

This step of describing the app may include the creation of visual mockups, wireframes or even prototypes. If it helps in communicating your thoughts to the client, then do it.

I've used wireframes and nonfunctional prototypes for most of my projects. These prototypes proved to be extremely useful. Especially if the client was not familiar with the platform or he had no precise expectations.

Let's say a customer asks you to create an iOS version of their Android app. A prototype will help the client understand that the iOS version will look and behave differently.

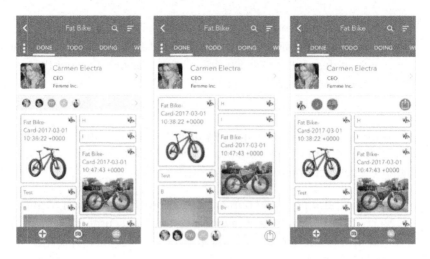

By communicating our vision precisely, we avoid surprises and false expectations.

Next comes the third phase. During this step, we aim to **identify the things that form our system**. These are the potential players that have a specific, well-defined role in our application.

Picking the essential entities won't be challenging if we did a good job at the previous two steps. We'll realize that we need a class that represents say an item that has a name, a price, and some other attributes; or a class responsible for securely communicating with a server. Another class may manage your local persistence, and so on.

In the final phase, we **describe the behavior of our system** in a formal way. This last step is about creating visual representations of our classes, their attributes and behavior. We also model the interaction between the objects.

We'll rely on the **Unified Modeling Language**, in short, UML. UML is a graphical notation that provides a set of standard diagrams. These diagrams let us describe object-oriented systems in a standard way.

This may sound overwhelming now, but no worries. We're going to discuss each of these concepts in the upcoming chapters.

DON'T PANIC

AND ALWAYS KNOW
WHERE YOUR TOWEL IS

The initial step of building a software system is crucial. It's often called **requirement collection phase** or **requirements analysis**. But regardless of how we call it, it paves the road for all the other phases of the object-oriented software design.

Requirement means "a thing that is needed or wanted." And exactly that's what we need to focus on during this initial step:

We must clarify what's needed or wanted in our application.

The features of the system are the so-called **functional requirements**. Functional requirements represent what the app needs to provide feature-wise, how it should react to a particular input, or what's the expected behavior in a specific situation.

Let's say you're about to develop an app for runners. You should answer questions like:

- Should the actual speed always be visible on the main screen?
- Do we allow imperial and metric units?
- Should we make this configurable by the user? Or automatically adjust the units based on the phone's settings instead?

iRun   Functional requirements

Show speed   Metric/Imperial   Customizable
                       Units

We'll usually also have **nonfunctional requirements**. These are the requirements that are not directly related to a feature or behavior of the software system but are important, nevertheless.

Think of performance requirements: you don't want to ruin the user experience with an unresponsive app. Also, you may need to address legal requirements. Does the app collect sensitive user data? Does it allow users to browse the internet?

Documentation and support are also nonfunctional requirements. Your software may need to adhere to certain standards or regulations.

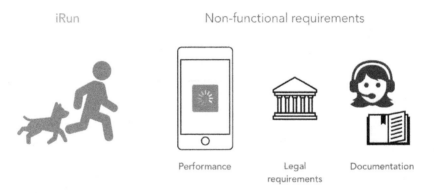

Nonfunctional requirements are equally important. Ignoring them may cause serious legal issues and all sorts of other problems.

Now, how do we handle this? There are different ways to gather the requirements. The easiest way is just to write them down. Here's an example from a project I've been working on.

Functional requirements

- The app must store travel expenses organized by trips.
- Each trip must have a home currency. The default currency is fetched from the phone's settings. User setting must override the default home currency.
- Expenses can be entered in any of the supported currencies. The app must automatically convert the amounts to the home currency.

Nonfunctional requirements

- The app must run on iOS 9 and newer versions.
- The app must avoid unnecessary network roundtrips to reduce data roaming fees and preserve battery.
- The app must include the support email and the link to the app's website.

These are short, concise phrases in the form:

"The app/system must do something."

You don't want to write lengthy descriptions, and feel free to adapt this format to your needs.

You should use some electronic form, but at early stages, pen and paper or a whiteboard are also fine. Just make sure you store them somehow, for example by taking photos.

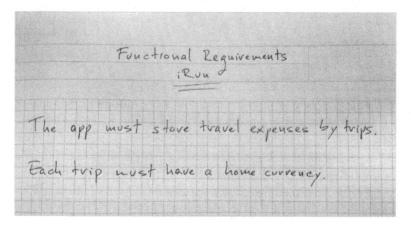

There are also more formal ways, tools, and systems that support the requirements collection step. I won't talk about these tools because this book is not about tools, but rather about principles.

To summarize, the requirements collection step boils down to this:

We need to formulate what our software must do and which are the constraints and boundaries we need to consider.

If we're using a Waterfall approach, we need to clarify all the requirements in advance.

For Agile projects, it's perfectly acceptable if we continue without having all the answers. We may even miss some of the questions. Agile lets us revisit and refine the requirements as we iterate through the software development process.

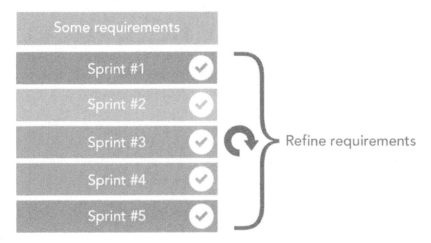

SECTION 4.2
MAPPING REQUIREMENTS TO TECHNICAL DESCRIPTIONS

Once we've gathered the requirements, we can feed them to the next step of the software design process. This is where we provide short, accurate descriptions of our system's functionality from the user's perspective.

One way of documenting our system's features is through use-cases. A use-case needs a title. Something like "Create New Trip," "Edit Expense" or "Convert Currencies." Note that each use-case should represent a distinct functionality.

Next, we define the actor who's using this functionality. We call it an "actor" since it can represent a user who's interacting with the app, but also a non-human entity, like another system.

Then, we describe the details of this specific use-case. This is called the scenario.

Here we should write one or more sentences that explain what and how the system works in this particular case. Here's an example:

Create new trip - this is the title of our use case. The actor is the user of the mobile app.

- The user can initiate the creation of a new trip from the main screen.
- The title is mandatory. All the other settings are optional.
- Optionally, the user can write a short description and set a start and end date for the trip.
- The app assigns a default home currency based on the phone's settings. Users can override the default home currency with any of the supported currencies.
- The app allows setting a budget for the trip. This setting is optional.
- Also, the user can assign a custom thumbnail to a trip.

- And the user can save the trip or cancel the trip creation process.

You can write this as a paragraph or as a bulleted list. The format doesn't really matter. But it's important to avoid technical terms. Again, this description should be understood by all stakeholders, including the end users.

The format of the use-case document may vary from company to company. Some may include additional details, but that won't change the essence of it.

The use-case document aims to provide a clear and human-friendly description. What a specific part of the software does and how the actor interacts with it. And this is a textual description. We'll talk about the use-case diagrams later.

User stories are another common way of describing certain features or parts of our application. User stories are shorter than use-case descriptions, usually only one-two sentence long. They typically follow this format:

As a < type of user >, I want < some goal > so that < some reason >.

Examples:

"As a user, I want to add notes to my expenses, so that I can identify them later on."

"As a power user, I want to retrieve the app's database file, so that I can inspect it on any computer."

If you can't describe a user story in one or two sentences, you may need to split it into multiple, smaller user stories. These larger user stories are known as **epics**. Epics cover a bigger chunk of functionality, like in the following case:

"As a traveler, I want to track my expenses while abroad, so that I don't exceed my budget."

This epic could be split into many user stories including these:

"As a user, I want to create new trips, so that I can track each of my travels separately."

"As a business traveler, I want to tag my business trips, so that I can separate them from my private travels."

User stories are often written on sticky notes or index cards. You'll see them arranged on walls or tables during meetings and discussions.

Unlike use-case descriptions, user stories don't capture the feature details. They serve as discussion starters instead.

User stories are about communication, and you'll usually see them in agile projects. Whereas use-case descriptions are preferably used by Waterfall methodologies.

The first two steps of the object-oriented analysis don't require any special tool or design language.

We only need some text-editing software. Even a piece of paper or a whiteboard would be sufficient to collect the requirements and jot down the use-cases or user stories.

The next steps require us to depict the classes that form our system. How they behave and what attributes they need.

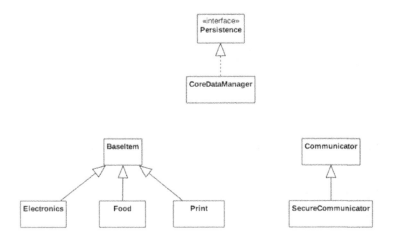

We also need to visualize how the objects interact with each other.

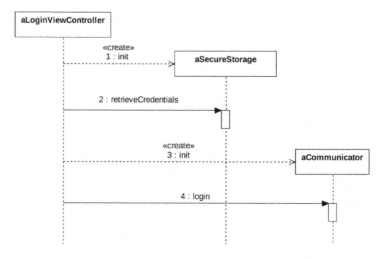

The development community faced this very same problem. The lack of a commonly accepted design language lead to the proliferation of different nonstandard approaches.

We could also try to come up with a way to draw everything from classes to object interactions. Luckily, we don't have to.

The **Unified Modeling Language** is a common design language that was released in 1997. UML provides a set of standard diagram types that can be used to describe both the structure and the behavior of software systems.

We'll dig deeper into UML in the upcoming section.

CHAPTER 5
UML BASICS AND FUNDAMENTAL DIAGRAM TYPES

Understanding a software system just by looking at its source code can be very time-consuming. And communicating ideas about software design or business processes is even harder if there's no commonly accepted way to do it.

The Unified Modeling Language - in short UML - was introduced to solve this problem. UML is not a textual programming language, but rather a graphical notation; a set of diagrams that help in designing and communicating software systems.

We can use these diagrams to describe the objects that form a system and their interactions. UML has many diagram types. We'll be discussing the most common ones.

The use-case diagram describes the functional model of a system. That is, the functionality of a system from the user's point of view.

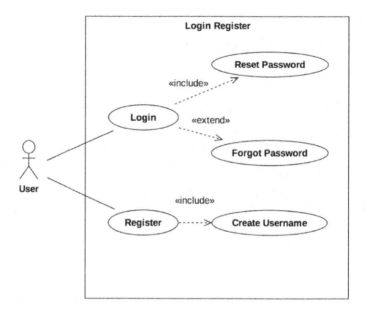

To describe the structure of a system, UML provides structural diagrams. We'll talk about the class diagram, which can be used to describe the structure of a system   in terms of objects, attributes, operations, and relations.

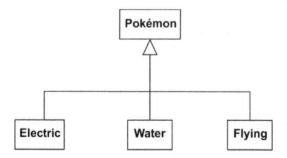

UML lets us model dynamic behavior, too. The behavioral diagrams describe the functionality of the system, focusing on what happens and the interactions between objects.

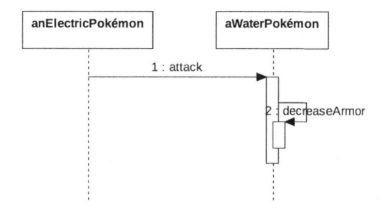

We'll talk about the actual diagrams shortly.

The best part about UML is that it's independent of any particular programming language. We can start coding an object-oriented software based on UML diagrams. If those diagrams are detailed enough, they can be converted to source code.

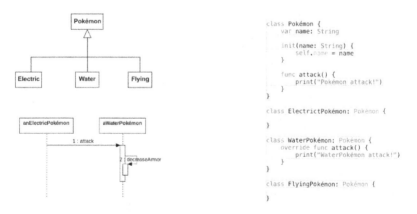

Now, let's see some ways of using UML in real-life. We can quickly draw a diagram to **sketch a specific part of a software or a new functionality.** I did that myself on numerous occasions. Whenever something was unclear, I started to sketch UML diagrams before writing a single line of code.

The benefit was that I not only understood what I should implement, I also had a design. A documentation that could be used to communicate my ideas with other team members.

Another frequent use of UML is drawing diagrams from existing code. This technique is called **reverse engineering**, and it helps to understand and document a system.

We can also use UML to **create the detailed blueprint of a system**. While sketches focus only on the essential aspects of a system, the blueprint is about completeness. Detailed UML blueprints are usually required for software developed using a Waterfall-approach - and less frequently for Agile projects.

You can use UML diagrams to describe any system that's developed using an object-oriented programming language. UML has become so popular that it's also used for non-object-oriented projects.

Let's start with the use-case diagram. It's one of the simplest UML diagrams.

Its purpose is to visualize the functional requirements of the system. Use-case diagrams show groups of related use-cases. Sometimes they may include all the use-cases.

The result is an overview of the system that may include several written use-cases. You'll rarely create use-case diagrams for a single use-case description.

To represent a use-case, we draw an oval in the middle of the screen and put the title of the use case in it.

"Create a Trip Entry," "Edit Trip," "Export App Database" - these are examples of use-cases from our Travel Expense app mentioned before.

We use stick figures to represent the actors. As you may recall, actors are human beings or other systems that may interact with our system.

We draw the stick person to the left or the right of the diagram. The actor's name goes below the stick figure.

Actor Name

We usually draw the primary actors on the left side and the secondary ones on the right side of the use-case diagram.

Next, we draw lines to represent the interaction between an actor and a use-case. A mobile user can create or edit a trip entry, but he cannot export the app's database. The power user can perform all these actions.

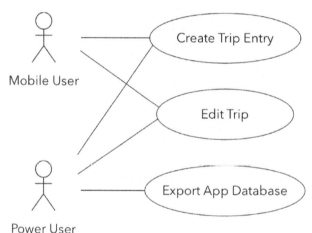

We need to visualize our system's boundaries if it interacts with other systems. For that, we draw a frame around all use-cases and actors that belong to a given system.

Let's say that we're relying on an external iCloud-based storage. I'll represent this external system as a separate actor on the right side. I even changed its visual representation to show that it's not a human actor. Most tools allow you to do that.

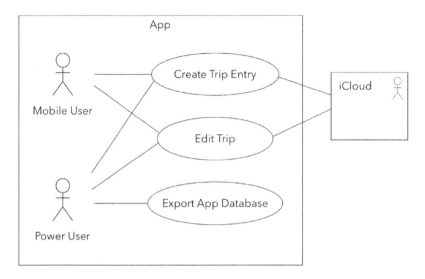

The "Create a Trip Entry" and the "Edit Trip" use cases would rely on the cloud to back up their data. So, I connect these use-cases with the external system.

The frame makes it obvious where our app's boundaries end. Use-case diagrams provide a clear way to communicate the high-level features and the scope of the system.

You can quickly tell what our system does just by looking at this use-case diagram.

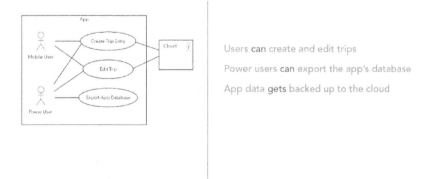

Users can create and edit trips

Power users can export the app's database

App data gets backed up to the cloud

This system lets users create new trips and edit existing ones. Power users can even export the database. The app relies on an external cloud system to store its data.

Such a simple diagram makes it clear what the system does and what it doesn't do. A customer or a user can easily see if needed features are missing. The absence of use cases shows what the system doesn't do.

The UML use-case diagram includes other artifacts and relationships between use-cases. We're going to ignore them as they tend to overcomplicate our design and the benefits are questionable.

You can't go wrong if you focus on the actors, the use-cases, and their interactions. You'll be able to easily create your own use-case diagrams and communicate your ideas in a clear and concise way.

Use-case diagrams provide an easy-to-understand overview of the features of our system.

They are not a replacement for written use-case descriptions, though. Use-case descriptions include more information to ensure that we don't miss any of the important details or requirements.

Without any doubt, class diagrams are the most frequently used UML diagram types. After identifying the entities that form our system, we start creating class diagrams for each of them.

A class is represented on the class diagram as a rectangle with three compartments. First, we need to list the class's name.

ClassName

When naming our classes, we must adhere to some rules. These rules are known as naming conventions. A class name should be a noun in the singular, and it needs to start with an uppercase letter.

If the name consists of multiple words, we need to uppercase each word, like in this example:

OfflinePersistenceManager

This style is called UpperCamelCase, which is CamelCase with the first letter capitalized.

CamelCase is the practice of starting each word in a compound word or sentence with a capital.

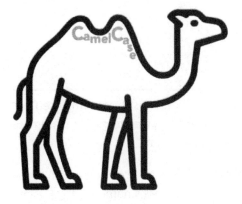

Why do we need rules? Why can't we just use any character sequence to name our classes? Well, we could do that.

Yet, a naming convention lets us focus on important issues instead of arguing over syntax and names. With a commonly accepted set of rules, we can easily read the source code written by other developers, even if they're from another company, country or continent. Standards are useful.

All right, so **our class name should be a noun in UpperCamelCase**. Let's fill the other two compartments, too. The next one lists the attributes.

The attribute names should be concise, and they should follow the lowerCamelCase format, that is, with the first letter lowercase and the first letters of subsequent words in uppercase.

Trip
name createdAt homeCurrency startsAt endsAt

A Trip has a name, it has a creation date (*createdAt*); it needs to have a home currency (*homeCurrency*), a start date (*startsAt*) and an end date (*endsAt*).

It's useful to specify the type of the attribute. We can do that by writing the data type after the attribute's name separated by a colon. So, here's our Trip class with the attribute names and types:

Trip
name: **String**
createdAt: **Date**
homeCurrency: **String**
startsAt: **Date**
endsAt: **Date**

The data types need to be adjusted to whatever programming language you're using. This example makes perfect sense in Swift. For Objective-C, you may want to use different types, like *NSString* instead of *String* and *NSDate* for dates.

Even if we leave it as it is, nobody will have issues understanding that you refer to a String or a Date or an integer.

Next comes the operations compartment. This is where we list the class's methods. **Method names should be verbs in lowerCamelCase.**

Trip
name: **String**
createdAt: **Date**
homeCurrency: **String**
startsAt: **Date**
endsAt: **Date**
save() delete() undoChanges()

We can also specify method arguments. The parameters appear within the parenthesis as name-data type pairs, like in *setName(value: String)*.

Trip
name: **String** createdAt: **Date** homeCurrency: **String** startsAt: **Date** endsAt: **Date**
setName(value: **String**) save() delete() undoChanges()

To show that a method returns something, we add a colon after the closing parenthesis followed by the return type:

getName(): String

And we can also have methods that have arguments and a return type.

Trip
name: **String** createdAt: **Date** homeCurrency: **String** startsAt: **Date** endsAt: **Date**
getEntries(from: **Date**, to: **Date**): List getName(): **String** setName(value: **String**) save() delete()

getEntries(from: Date, to: Date): List takes two arguments called *fromDate* and *endDate*, both of type *Date*. The method returns a *List* of entries. This list could contain multiple values or just a single value, or it could even be empty. We don't specify this in our class diagram.

Now, let's talk about visibility. UML allows us control who can access the attributes and the methods of our classes.

We have the following visibility levels in UML:

- + means public visibility. A class method or attribute marked as public can be used by code outside of the object.
- - denotes private access. Private attributes and methods can only be used within the class that defines them. Elements marked as private can't be accessed directly from other classes.
- UML uses **#** to mark an element as protected. Protected visibility means that only child classes (and the defining class) will be able to access that attribute or method.
- ~ denotes package visibility, which makes sense in some programming languages that let us group our code into logical units and provide a namespace for this group. Using package visibility, we make our elements available within its enclosing package.

UML provides these visibility tags, but it's up to us to adapt it to the language we're using. There's one rule that's commonly applicable to all object-oriented languages:

Expose only as much as needed and hide everything else.

Class attributes will usually have private or protected access. We should provide public setters and getters instead of allowing everybody to access our class's data. This lets us control what the callers do with our class's attributes.

In our Trip class, we could make the name attribute public. Callers could set and retrieve it, which seems to work as expected.

Trip
+ name

But, what if we need to make sure that a Trip's name is never shorter than say three characters?

```
name.length >= 3
```

There's no way to enforce this requirement.

Another example. The trip's start date needs to be earlier than its end date. Yet, callers can freely set any start or end date.

Trip
+ name +startsAt +endsAt

```
name.length >= 3
endsAt >= startsAt
```

I'm going to change the visibility of all these attributes to private. Now, we can access them exclusively from within the class's own methods. After this change, other objects can't set or retrieve these attributes. They are, well, private to the Trip class.

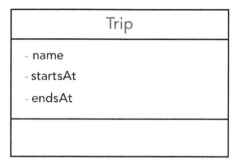

Awesome! But then, how do we set, retrieve or modify them?

Here's the solution: I provide public getters and setters for each of these attributes:

Trip
- name
- startsAt
- endsAt
+getName(): String +setName(value: String) +getStartDate(): Date +setStartDate(date: Date) +getEndDate(): Date +setEndDate(date: Date)

Now we can check whether the name is at least three characters long by validating the name parameter in the *setName()* method. If it's shorter, we just print a warning message and return.

```
class Trip {
    public func setName(value: String) {
        if value.count < 3 {
            print("Name too short!")
            return
        }
        //...
    }
}
```

}

Also, we validate the start and the end date in the corresponding setters.

```
public func setStartDate(date: Date) {
    if date > endDate {
        print("Trip's start date > end date")
        return
    }
    //...
}


public func setEndDate(date: Date) {
    if date < startDate {
        print("Trip's end date < start date")
        return
    }
    //...
}
```

We are now in full control of our class's internal data. Setters let us check the input argument, and getters allow us to modify the value before returning it. For example, we could return a date in the user's time zone.

So far, we've seen how to represent a single class. Class diagrams let us also show the relationships between the classes in our system. We'll talk about relationships next.

ASSOCIATIONS

The next logical step after identifying the key classes in our system is figuring out the relationships between them. Use-cases or user stories will help us during this process.

Here's one of the functional requirements of the TravelExpense app.

"As a traveler, I want to track my expenses while abroad, so that I don't exceed my budget."

We have a Trip and an Expense class. Each trip will include it's travel expenses. So, there needs to be some relationship between the Trip and the Expense class.

To express this relationship, we draw a solid line between these classes.

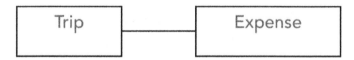

This line represents an association. The association tells us that the classes refer to each other.

We can be more specific here. The Trip class needs to know about its expenses. Should the Expense class also know about the Trip class?

We've already talked about the drawbacks of tightly coupled systems. Tight coupling is something that you should definitely try to avoid. Let me illustrate the issue it causes.

The Trip refers to the Expense class. That's fine, since a trip can have expenses associated with it. What happens if also the Expense refers to the Trip class?

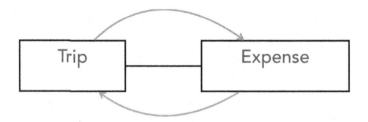

Because of this reference, if we tried to use the Expense class in other parts of the system, we'd need to also bring the Trip class with it.

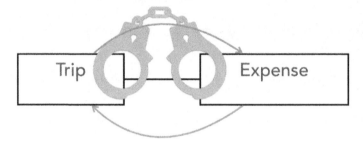

This doesn't make sense, as we should be able to use an Expense without a Trip.

UML lets us express directed associations. By drawing a solid line that ends with an open arrowhead, we show that only one of the classes refers to the other one. The arrow points to the class that's referred to by the other class.

In our current example, the association is bi-directional. Let's change it to a directed association.

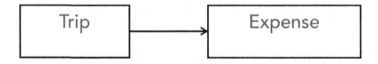

Now it shows that the Expense is associated with the Trip, but the Expense class doesn't know anything about the Trip class.

A Trip will usually have multiple expenses. We can represent the multiplicity of associated objects as follows:

- - a Trip can have zero or more Expenses

- 1 - a Trip must have exactly one homeCurrency
- 0..1 - a Trip may or may not have a single note

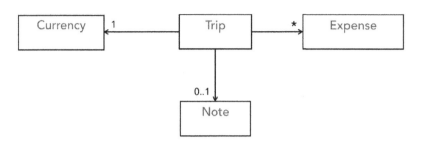

Associations can show multiplicities at both ends of the line. The default multiplicity is one. So, if there's no multiplicity shown, you can safely assume it's one.

We can also display the name of the class property for the given association.

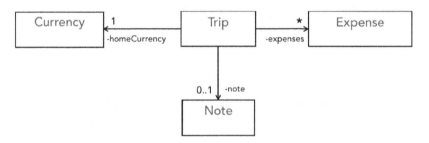

The association isn't the only kind of relationship we can have between classes. Next, we're going to talk about generalization.

In UML, we use generalization to express that one model element is based on another model element. Generalization is represented as a solid line with a hollow arrowhead that points to the parent.

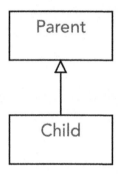

Let's say that we need a special *Trip* class for our business trips. *BusinessTrip* would inherit from the Trip class and this is how we represent it in UML:

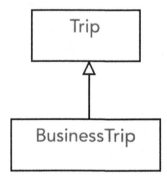

Because *BusinessTrip* inherits everything from its parent, we must only specify the attributes and operations that are specific to the child.

A parent can have multiple children.

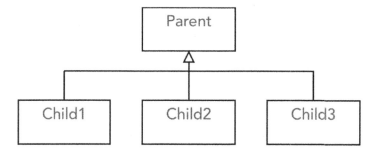

And we can also have child classes that inherit from different parents.

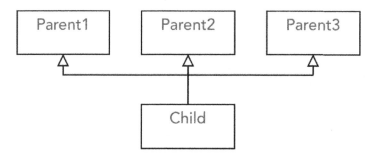

Some programming languages support multiple inheritance; C++, Perl, Python - just to name a few.

Many modern programming languages only allow single inheritance, that is, inheriting from one parent class. Single inheritance reduces the complexity and avoids the ambiguity that comes with multiple inheritance.

Some argue that multiple inheritance has more benefits than drawbacks. However, it's certainly easier to make mistakes when using multiple inheritance.

UML doesn't restrict generalization to classes. It can also be used in use-case or component diagrams. This lets us indicate that a child element receives it's parent's attributes, operations and relationships.

DEPENDENCY, AGGREGATION, COMPOSITION AND REALIZATION

DEPENDENCY

We talk about a dependency relationship if changes in one of the classes may cause changes to the other.

In UML, dependency is represented as a dashed line that ends with an open arrowhead. The arrow points to the dependency.

A dependency is a directed relationship.

Dependency is often confused with Association, but there's a big difference. Association indicates that a class has an attribute of the other class's type.

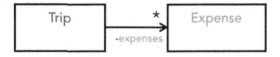

association

Whereas dependency is usually created when a class receives a reference to the other class (for instance, through a member function parameter).

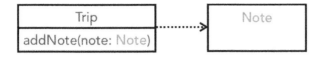

dependency

AGGREGATION AND COMPOSITION

Aggregation represents a part-whole relationship and is drawn as a solid line with a hollow diamond at the owner's end.

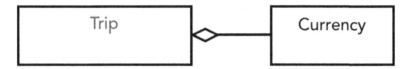

This relationship is considered redundant because it expresses the same thing as the association. So, these two diagrams are equivalent:

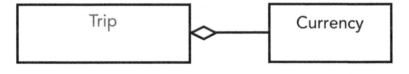

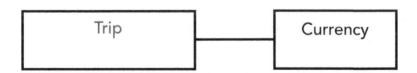

Composition is a stronger form of association. It shows that the parts live and die with the whole. In other words, composition implies ownership: when the owning object is destroyed, the contained objects will be destroyed, too.

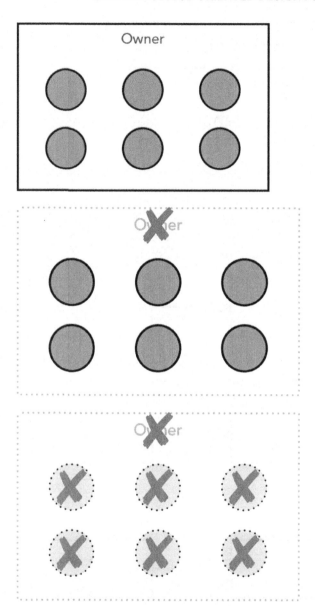

The composition is represented as a filled diamond on the owner's end connected with a solid line with the contained class.

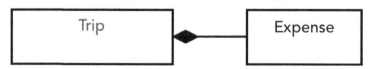

The Expenses of a trip can't exist without the Trip. If we delete the Trip instance,

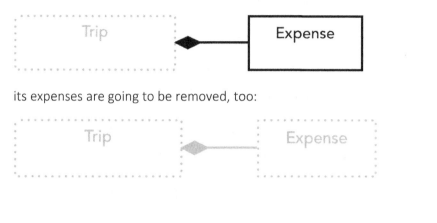

its expenses are going to be removed, too:

REALIZATION

Realization indicates that a class implements the behavior specified by another model element.

It is represented as a hollow triangle on the interface end connected with dashed lines with the implementer classes.

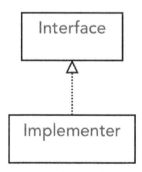

We could specify an interface to ensure that all current and upcoming trip classes provide a common set of methods. This is a useful feature that allows polymorphic behavior.

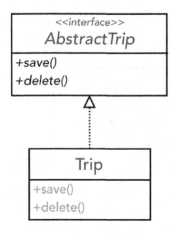

Here's a quick summary of the relationships and their graphical representation:

Generalization /
"is-a"

Association /
"has-a"

Aggregation /
"has-a"

Composition /
"part-of"

Dependency /
"references"

Realization /
"implements behavior"

SEQUENCE DIAGRAMS

Use case and class diagrams are static diagrams. They are great at representing the structure of our system.

What if we need to show how the objects interact with each other? When are objects created and for how long are they around? Static diagrams can't answer these questions.

UML provides dynamic diagrams to represent how objects communicate with each other. The most common dynamic diagram is the sequence diagram.

We use the sequence diagram to describe the flow of logic in one particular scenario.

A sequence diagram starts by drawing boxes at the top of the page. Each box represents an object. Since these are objects, we name them differently. "aTrip" instead of "Trip" and "anExpense" rather than "Expense."

aTrip	anExpense

We can also display the type after the instance's name separated by a colon. This may be helpful in some cases:

aTrip: Trip	anExpense: Expense

The lifeline of an object is represented by the dotted lines beneath each box. This line shows the time the instance exists during the scenario.

The sequence diagram also lets us show the messages sent from one object to the other. A message is basically a method call.

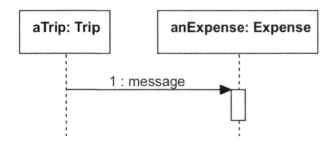

Now, let me illustrate the various messages in a practical example. I'll be using StarUML, a UML diagramming software that can be downloaded for free from www.staruml.io.

Let's assume that we have a *persistenceManager* object. This object is responsible for storing and retrieving entities in the app's local database.

The *persistenceManager* needs to create and store a *TripEntity* instance. First, I add the *TripEntity* object. The *persistenceManager* instance sends a create message to initiate a *tripEntity* object. The create message is represented as a dashed line with a stick arrowhead.

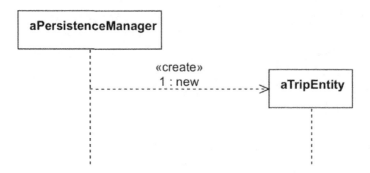

Next, the *persistenceManager* sends a regular message to the already created trip entity. This message corresponds to calling the *addNote(note: String)* method on the *TripEntity* instance. A regular message is shown as a solid line with a filled arrowhead. We can add parameters to our messages if we wish:

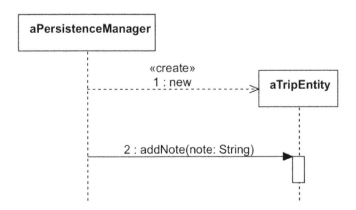

Although we could display the return message, only do it if it's important. Return messages are implicit for synchronous messages, so we don't have to display them.

Asynchronous messages are drawn as solid lines with a stick arrowhead. The controller object sends an asynchronous *save(trip: Trip)* message to the *persistenceManager*. Disk operations are slow, so inserting a new record into the database is a perfect candidate for an asynchronous call.

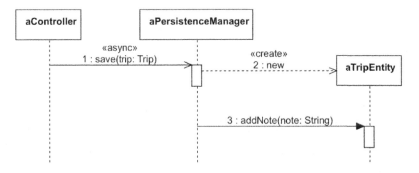

When an object sends any async message, it doesn't need to wait for a response. The asynchronous call gets executed in the background, and it returns once it completes. Unlike synchronous calls, it doesn't block the caller.

Asynchronous behavior stands at the core of modern software systems. They improve responsiveness on multicore processors and provide better user experience because lengthy operations won't block the user interface.

So, you'll probably draw async messages a lot.

The issue is that the difference between regular and async messages is very subtle: stick arrowhead instead of a filled arrowhead. To avoid misunderstanding, you can add an extra note to make it visible it's an async message.

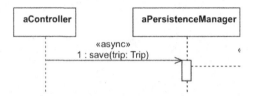

We also have self-messages. These represent a method calling another method of the same object.

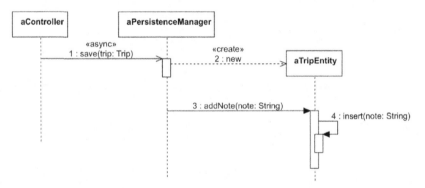

An object can also send a delete message to another object. The *persistenceManager* sends a delete message to the tripEntity instance.

The TripEntity gets destroyed, and its lifeline gets terminated by a cross symbol.

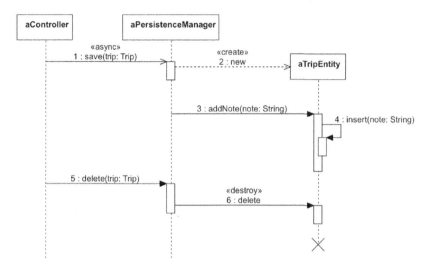

Sequence diagrams should provide an overview of what's going on in a given scenario. We don't try to represent all the method calls precisely. Instead, we focus on the most relevant parts.

Sequence diagrams help us in clarifying the interactions between objects in a specific scenario. By getting more profound insights into the inner workings of our objects, we may need to refine their behavior. Or even add new classes or establish new relationships between our classes.

And that's perfectly fine. The process of designing a software system is all about finding out what's missing, what needs to be enhanced or changed.

Activity diagrams can be used to describe workflows. The actions are represented by nodes. We start an activity diagram with an initial node drawn as a small, filled circle. We can then transition to the next node. The transition is called flow, and it's shown as a line that ends with an open arrowhead. The arrow points the direction of the logic flow from one action to the other.

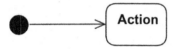

Activity diagrams can also express conditional logic. We model a decision node as a diamond. It has a single incoming flow and two or more outbound flows.

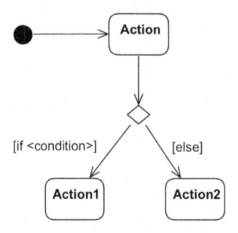

Each outbound flow has a *guard*, which is a Boolean condition placed inside square brackets. The guards need to be mutually exclusive. Whenever we reach a decision, we can choose only one of the outbound flows.

After a decision, the flows can be merged using a merge activity. A merge has multiple input flows and a single output flow.

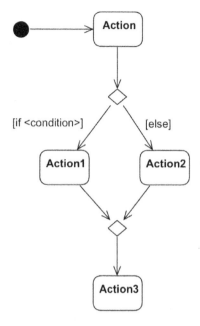

Activity diagrams support parallel behavior. To express concurrent flows, we use a fork drawn as a thick horizontal line. A fork has one incoming flow and several outgoing concurrent flows.

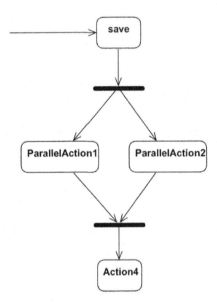

We need to synchronize the tasks that execute concurrently. For example, we can't display the image while it's being read from the local persistence or downloaded from the server. A join represents a synchronization point.

The final node represents the end of the workflow.

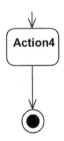

The following activity diagram describes a simplified version of the trip creation process.

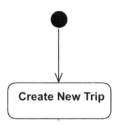

We begin with the initial node. The user decides to create a new trip.

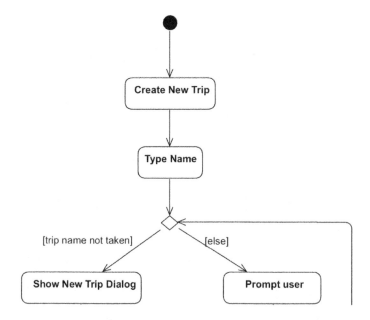

Next, he's asked to type the trip's name. Now, the app needs to check whether a trip with the same name already exists.

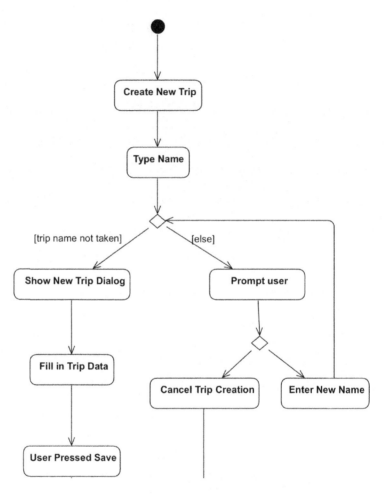

If it does, we prompt the user to enter a new name or cancel the trip creation process. If he decides to cancel the flow, we end the activity. Otherwise, we validate the name again.

If the trip name isn't taken, we let the user fill the remaining trip data. Finally, the user hits the save button. We may also want to let him cancel the process here.

Now, I'll use a fork to show that we perform some actions in parallel. Storing the new trip into the local persistence and uploading it to the cloud server happen concurrently.

If both actions succeed, we inform the user about the successful trip creation, and we're done.

We can add more details and further actions to our activity diagram if that's useful.

The activity diagram is a useful technique to represent behavioral logic. I wouldn't recommend it when working with nontechnical people, though.

SECTION 5.9
STATECHART DIAGRAMS

The Statechart or State Machine diagram models how an object transitions from one state to another over its lifetime.

It describes the state changes of an object in response to certain events.

A state is a condition in which an object exists. Think of object states like *New*, *Pending Changes* or *Completed*.

These states can change when some event gets triggered. The *Pending Changes* state transitions to *Saved* after a successful save event.

And the *Saved* state will change to the final *Terminated* state if the object is deleted.

The state machine diagram starts with an initial state. This is not a real state, but rather the entry point. States are drawn as rectangles with rounded corners with the state's name. The transitions from one state to another are shown as lines that end in an open arrow.

Each transition can be labeled with an event name and a guard.

The guard appears between angle brackets; it's a Boolean condition that needs to be true for the state change to occur.

Let's assume that pending changes can only be saved if the device is connected to the internet. We can represent conditional logic in statechart diagrams as follows:

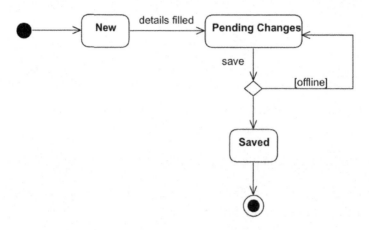

The final state shows that the state machine is completed, and it also implies the deletion of the object.

Use statechart diagrams to describe the object states of a system while identifying the events responsible for the state changes.

CHAPTER 6
CASE STUDY: DESIGNING A NOTE-TAKING APP

In this chapter, I walk you through the process of designing a note-taking application.

We'll start by collecting the requirements and writing user stories. We're going to analyze the system from various angles. By the end of this chapter, we'll have created several UML diagrams that describe the structure and the behavior of our software.

This is going to be an interesting exercise as we put into practice what we learned so far.

SECTION 6.1
COLLECTING THE REQUIREMENTS

In this lecture, I'm going to illustrate the requirements collection phase through a real example.

Let's start by thinking about the features of a note-taking application. First, we're going to be creating and editing text-based notes. But we don't want to create the next boring note-taking app.

So, let's get creative and add some interesting features.

How about adding photos to our notes? And capturing hand-drawn sketches would be a cool addition, too.

Privacy has become increasingly important. We should allow the storing of sensitive notes.

Automatic syncing to Dropbox, iCloud or Google Drive? Sure, many users will find that a useful feature.

Now that we have some ideas floating around, we can come up with a first draft of our distilled requirements.

Note-Taking App - Functional Requirements

- We need to build a note-taking app. Users can create and edit text-based notes. A note may also include images or hand-drawn sketches.
- Sensitive notes can be protected from prying eyes using a password.
- The app automatically uploads changes to pre-configured servers. We should support all major platforms: Dropbox, iCloud and Google Drive.

Next, let's talk about the nonfunctional requirements.

Note-Taking App - Nonfunctional Requirements

- Let's release our app for iOS first. We'll support iOS 10 and newer versions. The app needs to run on the iPhone and the iPad as well.
- We'll create a dedicated support website and include the link in the app's description and its "About" page.
- Now that we have collected the requirements, we can proceed to the next step. We're going to map these requirements to technical descriptions.

SECTION 6.2
CREATING USER STORIES

Now that we've gathered the requirements, we'll be writing user stories. So, let's get started.

These are the functional requirements:

Note-Taking App - Functional Requirements

- We need to build a note-taking app. Users can create and edit text-based notes. A note may also include images or hand-drawn sketches.
- Sensitive notes can be protected from prying eyes using a password.
- The app automatically uploads changes to pre-configured servers. We should support all major platforms: Dropbox, iCloud and Google Drive.

Considering these requirements, we identify three major topics:

1. Note creation and editing
2. Privacy - protecting user data
3. Syncing to cloud servers

These are all big chunks of functionality that can't be described through single user stories. Thus, I'm going to create an epic for each. As you may recall, an epic consists of multiple user stories that describe common functionality.

Epic #1: Note creation and editing

- As a user, I want to create and edit notes so that I can quickly jot down my thoughts.
- As a user, I want to attach photos to a note so that I can keep my memories in one place.
- As a user, I want to add handwritten sketches so that I can insert funny drawings into my notes.

Epic #2: Privacy - Protecting User Data

- As a user, I want to create private notes so that only I can access them.
- As a user, I want to protect my sensitive notes with a password.

Epic #3: Syncing to cloud servers

- As a user, I want to sync my notes across my iOS devices so that my data is up-to-date on all of them.
- As a user, I want my notes automatically uploaded to cloud servers (Dropbox, Google Drive or iCloud) so that I have a backup of all my data.

These user stories are technical descriptions that serve as a starting point for our use-case diagrams. Up next, I'm going to show how we might go ahead and map these user stories to actual use-case diagrams.

In this lecture, we're going to represent our user stories as use-case diagrams. Let's start with the first epic:

Epic #1: Note creation and editing

- As a user, I want to create and edit notes so that I can quickly jot down my thoughts.
- As a user, I want to attach photos to a note so that I can keep my memories in one place.
- As a user, I want to add handwritten sketches so that I can insert funny drawings into my notes.

Let's map these user stories to a use-case diagram.

The actor is the user of this app. Next, I add the use-cases: "Create Note" and "Edit Note".

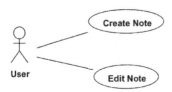

We also need an "Attach Photo" and "Add Handwritten Sketch" use case. Now, these are not standalone use-cases. We can't attach a photo or add a handwritten sketch without creating or editing a note. Thus, I represent them as included in the "Create Note" and "Edit Note" use-cases.

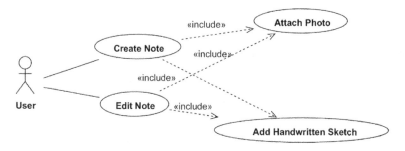

Let's continue with the second epic.

Epic #2: Privacy - Protecting User Data

- As a user, I want to create private notes so that only I can access them.
- As a user, I want to protect my sensitive notes with a password.

Again, we need an actor; it's the user as usual.

The creation of private notes is a special case of note creation. We can represent the "Create Private Note" as an extension of the regular "Create Note" use-case.

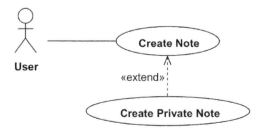

We need to protect sensitive notes with a password, so I create a "Protect with Password" use case for it. This use-case should be included in the Create Private Note use-case, so I draw it using an include relationship.

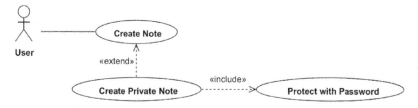

Here's the third epic:

Epic #3: Syncing to cloud servers

- As a user, I want to sync my notes across my iOS devices so that my data is up-to-date on all of them.
- As a user, I want my notes automatically uploaded to cloud servers (Dropbox, Google Drive or iCloud) so that I have a backup of all my data.

This epic is about synchronizing data with a server. This server is another actor, a non-human one. I'll represent it on the right side of the diagram using this special format.

Let's determine the use-cases. So, whenever we create or modify a note, it needs to be sync'd with the server.

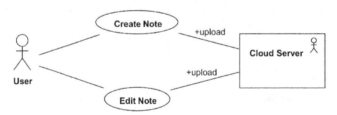

That's an over simplification, but it illustrates what needs to happen in this scenario. As you may recall, use-case diagrams are a means to share our ideas with nontechnical people, so try to keep it simple.

Next, we get into more technical details, as we'll start to identify our classes.

SECTION 6.4
IDENTIFYING THE CLASSES

Let's create the static structure of our system. We'll identify the main classes and the relationships between them.

Our app is about taking notes. So, we'll need a class that represents a Note.

A Note has a text. So, I add a private attribute called "text" of type String. As you may recall, we should not expose class properties. Hence "text" is private.

What else do we know? Let's take a look at the use-case diagrams we've put together.

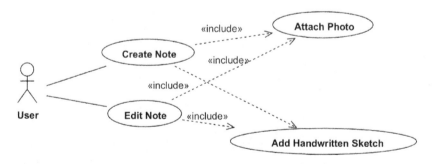

We also need an "Attach Photo" and "Add Handwritten Sketch" use case. A Note needs to have an attribute for the photos and one for the handwritten sketches.

I'm using the plural form: photos and sketches. That is, a Note may have many photos and hand-drawn sketches attached to it. So, I'll make these attributes of List type.

Note
-text: String -photos: List<Image> -sketches: List<Sketch>

The photos attribute is a List of Image type. I introduce an Image class, which can later be changed to an existing type. In iOS, that would be UIImage, but that's not important. The point is to identify the potential classes that play a role in our system.

Note		Image
-text: String -photos: List<Image> -sketches: List<Sketch>		

Similarly, we need a list of sketches. The Sketch class represents our hand-drawn sketches.

The Note class needs some methods:

- *addImage(image: Image)* to attach a new image and
- *getImages(): List<Image>* to retrieve all images of a Note.
- *addSketch(sketch: Sketch)* and
- *getSketches(): List<Sketch>* to get the hand-draw sketches of a Note

Note
-text: String -photos: List<Image> -sketches: List<Sketch>
+addImage(image: Image) +getImages(): List<Image> +addSketch(sketch: Sketch) +getSketches(): List<Sketch>

We don't know anything yet about the underlying format for the Image and the Sketch class.

And that's fine. We need to abstract things first and iteratively refine it. At the end, we may store our hand-drawn sketches either as a JPEG image. But requirements may change, and we'll need a vector format, so we'll use PDF.

Again, we should not go into such details at this stage or we may easily get stuck. This phenomenon is well-know and it even has a name: analysis-paralysis.

Start with a few broad strokes instead of overthinking and spending too much time on figuring out the details right away. Then try to get more specific as you understand more.

Now, let's think about the relationships between these classes. Is there an association between the Note and the Image class? Or rather a dependency?

The Note class has an attribute that refers to the Image and the Sketch class. It did not receive instances of these classes as parameters to a method, so it's not a dependency relationship.

So, is it an association? Yes, it is. But let's dig a bit deeper.

What happens when we delete a Note object with its images and sketches? They will be destroyed, too. It doesn't make sense to keep them if the user decides to remove the Note.

That means that the images and the sketches live and die with the Note object. As you may recall, this is the "part-of" relationship called composition.

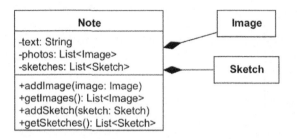

Now, an Image doesn't need to know about the Note. Nor does the Sketch. So, these are directed relationships.

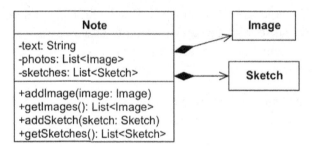

Based on the second epic, we need a specialized Note that holds sensitive data.

Epic #2: Privacy - Protecting User Data

- As a user, I want to create private notes so that only I can access them.
- As a user, I want to protect my sensitive notes with a password.

This note shares most of the attributes and behavior associated with the Note class. This looks like a perfect candidate for inheritance.

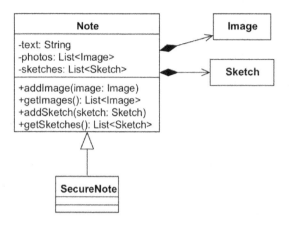

SecureNote inherits from the *Note* class.

In addition to the inherited attributes, it has a property called *passwordHash*.

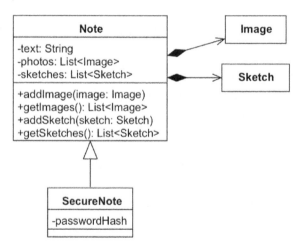

Storing the password is insecure. Instead, we store the password's hash value. The hash is generated using a one-way hashing algorithm from the password. The password can't be reconstructed from its hash value.

For the hashing algorithm, I'm going to define a *Crypto* class. It provides the public *hash()* method that takes a String as input and returns its hash value. The *SecureNote* is going to rely on the *Crypto* utility class to create the password hash. I indicate this as a dependency between the *SecureNote* and the *Crypto* class.

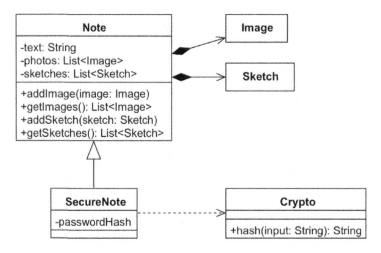

Next, we need a class that's responsible for storing the notes and their associated data in the local persistence. We don't want to be too specific at this point as we haven't defined yet what local persistence means. It could be the filesystem or an SQLite database. We could also choose CoreData.

That's not important at this point, so we'll use abstraction. Instead of specifying a concrete file or database manager, I'm going to create an interface that defines a couple of methods.

Let's call it *LocalPersistence*. It's an interface: it declares the method signatures that need to be implemented, but it provides no functionality. The implementation classes will be responsible for implementing these methods. The *LocalPersistence* declares the following interface:

- *getNotes(): List<Node>* - retrieves all notes from the local persistence
- *save(note: Note)* - stores a note locally
- *update(note: Note)* - updates a note that has been persisted
- *delete(note: Note)* - removes a note from the local persistence

All these methods have parameters or return values of type *Note*. Thus, we can draw a dependency relationship between the *LocalPersistence* interface and the *Note* class.

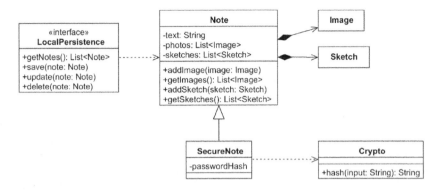

Let's say that we decide to store our notes in the file system. The *FileManager* implements the methods declared in *LocalPersistence*. I use the realization relationship to show that.

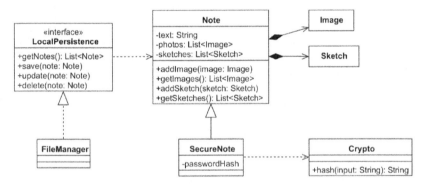

Similarly, I'll create an interface for the cloud syncing feature. The NetworkController interface declares the methods that take care of the networking-related operations*:

- *fetchNotes(): List<Node>* - fetches all notes from the server
- *upload(note: Note)* - uploads a new note to the server
- *refresh(note: Note)* - updates the note that has been uploaded
- *remove(note: Note)* - deletes a note from the server

Networking is slow, so these should be implemented as asynchronous operations.

(*)Network controllers are more complex but let's keep it simple for this example.

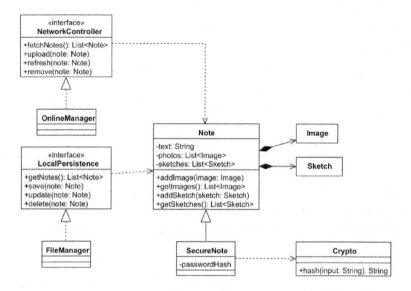

By now, you've probably got an idea of how class diagrams are created. Now that we mapped the static structure of our system, we can start analyzing its behavior.

SECTION 6.5
DESCRIBING THE FLOW OF NOTE CREATION USING SEQUENCE DIAGRAMS

I'm going to walk you through the creation of the sequence diagram for one specific scenario: adding a new note.

We'll be focusing on the flow of note creation. We try to answer the following question:

Which objects are involved and what messages are sent between them?

The user can initiate the note creation by pressing a button on the application's **user interface**. So, we need a view instance first that represents the button. The button receives the user input and triggers and event that's intercepted by a controller object.

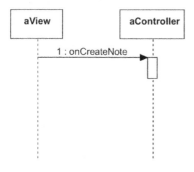

Having separate view and controller objects stands at the core of a well-known architectural design pattern called *Model-View-Controller*. The view displays data and receives user input. The controller triggers actions based on events received from its view and processes the data to be displayed.

In our scenario, the controller triggers the creation of a new *Note* instance. We'll use a create message rather than a regular one. A *Note* object gets created.

104

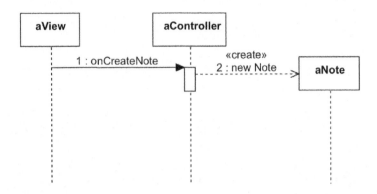

Next, the user fills the note's details and presses the save button. This will trigger two actions: saving to the local persistence and uploading the new note to the cloud.

Local persistence is managed by the *FileManager* object. I invoke the *save(note: Note)* method. File operations are slow, thus I call the save method asynchronously. To avoid misunderstanding, I mark the message explicitly as async.

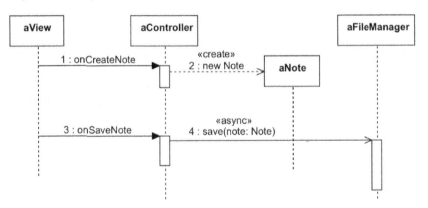

For the upload part, we need an *OnlineManager* instance. The *upload(note: Note)* method gets executed in the background, too.

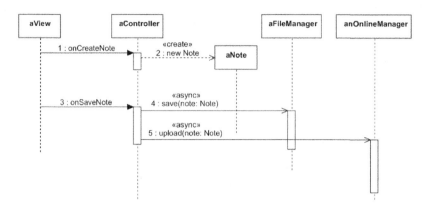

The saving to local persistence and uploading the new Note to the cloud are asynchronous, so they return instantly, without blocking the caller. Eventually, they return to signal either success or failure.

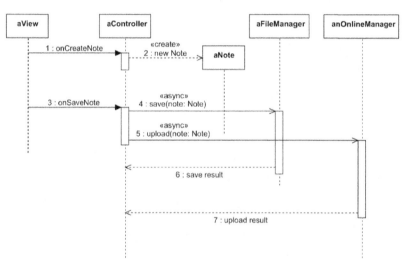

This sequence diagram tells us a lot about the objects and how they interact in the note creation scenario. We can provide more details by adding further objects and messages as needed.

THE NOTE OBJECT'S STATECHART DIAGRAM

Let's take a closer look at the possible states of a note object. A note object is created, saved and that's it, right? Well, not quite.

We start by analyzing the possible states and what could go wrong. We'll soon realize that we need to represent more states than we originally assumed.

The Note object's statechart diagram starts with an initial state. When we create a note, it's in the *New* state. This condition is triggered by the creation event.

After a new note is created, the user needs to fill in some details. At the end of this process, the note will have unsaved changes. We need a state to express this condition.

Now, the user can save the Note. He may also decide to cancel the process, which means that our state machine reached its final state.

Saving a note implies storing it in the local persistence and uploading it to the cloud. These are two actions that could potentially fail.

If both fail, the state of our Note object turns back to *Unsaved Changes*. Otherwise, we switch to the *Persisted & Uploaded* state.

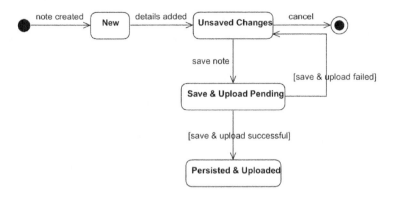

Storing a new note in the file system will usually complete without issues. However, uploading data to a server could fail for various reasons. The *Persisted* state shows that only the local storage was successful.

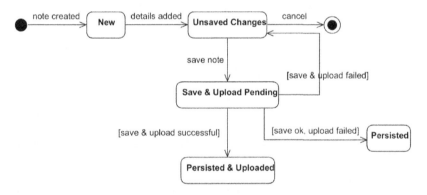

The user can retry the uploading action, which changes the state of the note object to *Upload Pending*. If this attempt also fails, we go back to the *Persisted* state. Otherwise, the object's state switches to *Persisted & Uploaded*.

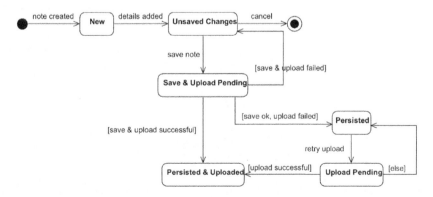

Our note object was successfully created, saved to the local persistence and uploaded to a cloud server. That's the last state so we can complete our state machine by transitioning to the final state.

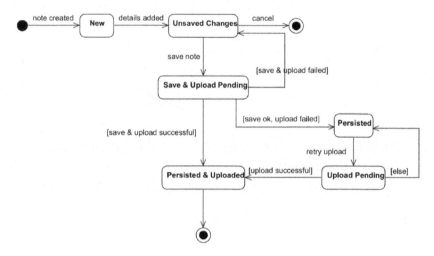

When creating statechart diagrams, it's important to always have a way to exit a state after it's entered. The only exceptions are the initial and the final states.

Let's say that I want to express the *Archived* state. The note object should switch to that state if the app is terminated while the note is in the *Unsaved Changes* state.

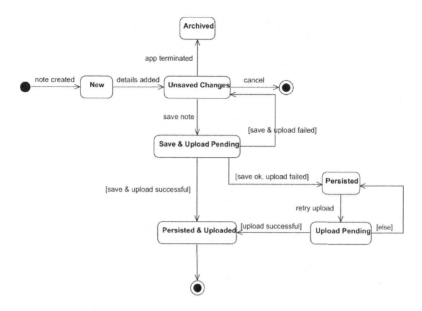

When the user starts the app next time, the note remains stuck in this *Archived* state. There's no transition to any other state. This situation is called **deadlock** and it's one of the biggest issues you can encounter with state machines.

To solve the problem, I add a transition to the *Unsaved Changes*. This transition is triggered by the *App Started* event.

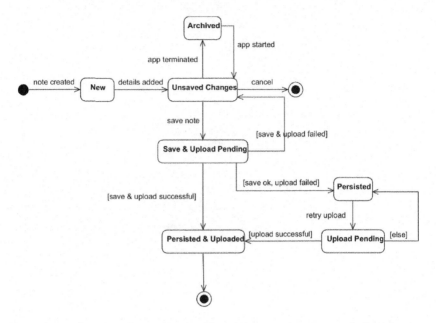

So, this is the statechart diagram for the note object. We definitely got more states than we originally assumed.

CHAPTER 7
WHAT'S NEXT?

Congrats, you've reached the end of this book!

By now, you've probably become familiar with the fundamental object-oriented design concepts.

Practice makes the master. Try to put the techniques described in this book into practice. You'll notice that designing software systems gets easier over time.

Explore different alternatives when sketching your designs. Although there are some best practices, feel free to adapt them to your needs.

And most importantly: Don't get lost in the details. Start with a simpler, draft design. You can gradually refine and enhance your diagrams as you understand more about the system you're building.

SECTION 7.1
GOODBYE!

I'd love to hear from you! Feel free to email me at carlos@leakka.com. And if you found this book useful, please leave a nice review or rating at https://www.amazon.com/dp/B079W497MZ .

Thank you!

As an instructor, my goal is to share my 20+ years of software development expertise. I've worked with companies such as Apple, Siemens, SAP, Zen Studios, and many more.

I'm teaching software development related topics, including object-oriented software design, iOS programming, Swift, Objective-C, and UML.

You can find my programming courses on **all the major platforms:**

Udemy: https://www.udemy.com/user/karolynyisztor

Lynda: https://www.lynda.com/Karoly-Nyisztor/9655357-1.html

LinkedIn: https://www.linkedin.com/learning/instructors/karoly-nyisztor

Pluralsight: https://www.pluralsight.com/profile/author/karoly-nyisztor

My books are available on **Amazon** amazon.com/author/nyisztor and **iTunes** https://itunes.apple.com/us/author/karoly-nyisztor/id1345964804?mt=11.

Check out these links for free tutorials, blog posts and other useful stuff:

Website: http://www.leakka.com

Youtube: https://www.youtube.com/c/swiftprogrammingtutorials

Github: https://github.com/nyisztor

Twitter: https://twitter.com/knyisztor

SECTION 7.3
COPYRIGHT

Made in the USA
Monee, IL
28 May 2022